A Timeless Moment

A journey into time and timelessness on Aldeburgh beach

Caroline Wiseman

For Francis

I took this photo of Francis as he was just about to give a speech at the Yorkshire Sculpture Park

'The most beautiful thing we can experience is the mysterious. It is the source of all true art and science.' Albert Einstein.

From stardust to stardust

"From stardust to stardust!" Steve cried out as he climbed down the long spiral staircase of our Lookout tower on Aldeburgh beach, after a long day of reading, writing, thinking and wondering.

The night before, Steve, Margaret, Francis and I did what human beings have done since we first became human. We looked into the night sky. We four, that night, were searching for shooting stars. And just like early humans before us, we were filled with wonderment. Even Steve. Especially Steve. He, like his fellow physicist Einstein, was awe struck by the mystery of the universe. 'We,' said Steve, that late afternoon, his voice fighting the crashing of the waves, the gentle roar of the wind and the crunching of pebbles beneath our feet, 'are 93 percent stardust, and we and everything else on this planet will return to stardust.'

Our Lookout tower from where we marvelled at the heavens stands on the beach in the pretty seaside town of Aldeburgh, in the county of Suffolk, on the east coast of England. Here the sea changes every moment – sometimes a soft turquoise, sometimes bluer, sometimes shades of taupe. Today, after a heavy storm, the suns shines on it so it shimmers and glistens like a sequinned camisole. Often it softly laps, sometimes it crashes loudly. The shingle beach is bleak and beautiful and also changes colour - last night before the storm it was apricot-orange. And this beach is where Britain's most eminent composer, Benjamin Britten, found a sense of spirituality, which he called the numinous. While he walked he composed the music for his opera about the sea, *Billy Budd.* The composer would discuss the big issues of life with his librettist, E M Forster when the writer came to visit him here in Aldeburgh in 1949. Forster told Britten that while he understood the attraction of the core principles of Christianity, such as tenderness, pity and love, he felt that religion was conditional on certain beliefs and behaviour. 'I have to find my emotional explanation of the universe, for of course I must find one, elsewhere,' he said.

Aldeburgh Beach is an ideal place to make that emotional journey. A couple of years before Professor Steve Cowley and his wife, the artist, Margaret Koval, came to visit Francis and me, I had been about to have a morning swim in Aldeburgh's North Sea when I noticed that a little lookout tower on the beach was for rent. While I swam my mind dissolved into a reverie – this little tower would be a tiny temple of creativity – for the town, the county, the country, the world!

We sold our London house, bought the tower and the handsome house which overlooks it, and Francis and I each began our quests, our own personal emotional explanations of the universe. For Francis it continued his lifelong response to the philosopher- theologian Soren Kierkegaard's challenge to us all to take seriously the inward experience of being human and explore and respond to life by discovering for ourselves our own personal spirituality. For me it was that and something very specific – I began an exploration into the enigma of human creativity. And my philosophical rendezvous with Steve that day gave me the impetus I needed to explore this elusive phenomenon with renewed vigour.

Time and timelessness

The Lookout tower stands bang in front of our house. It's there always to remind us of our quests. It's a tiny temple to art with spiral steps leading up to heaven. It's also (people say) like a tiny Tate, as most weeks a different artist takes possession of all three floors to create something completely new with which to wow us all on our Saturday openings to the public.

We moved here in 2010, and each day Francis and I would experience the ceaseless changing of the littoral, the shoreline, between the pebble beach and the sea. On our walks Francis would exclaim 'this is a timeless moment!' – his response to the sense of the numinous he, we, Britten and others feel here in this strange landscape. Our walks in the in-between of sea and land symbolized our search to understand our existence in the in-between of time and timelessness. Sometimes he would recite, as we walked, verses by one of his favourite poets, T S Eliot:

> Not known, because not looked for
> But heard, half heard, in the stillness
> Between two waves of the sea.

Francis slipped over a rug, we think, in the bathroom one morning, a few days before Christmas in 2014, and hit his head on the bidet. While I was unaware, thousands of feet in the air flying back from Peru, he was lying on the cold, wooden floor, unconscious, semi-conscious – who knows? – until lunchtime, when he was found by our cleaning lady. Bleeding seeped into his brain. Hydrocephalus developed.

Francis as we knew him was lost for ever.

Now Francis can still recite, on request, a few lines from T S Eliot; they seem to arise randomly from the depths somewhere of a less damaged part of his cerebral cortex. They are not perfectly remembered, as they once were, and it's not at all clear if he understands them, or anything about his life. We can no longer walk together along the littoral as I can't push his wheelchair over the pebbles.

Yet, I am pleased to say, awe and wonder still infuse life here on Aldeburgh beach. This sense of wonder has emotionally moved human beings since we animals developed the enigma of consciousness. Like T S Eliot and Francis (and me, even) humans, since the beginning of time, have searched for the meaning of the mystery of existence within this cosmic universe. We attempt to interpret our feeling of transcendence. For pre-modern humans, spirituality, art, cosmology and science were inseparable from life, it seems, each a way to try to gain a fuller, more complete understanding. But now, so sadly, science sits in a different camp to art and religion. And we humans are, too often, allocated, early on, one camp or the other. The Logos or the Mythos. The head or the heart. And the head, ruled by the left hemisphere of our brain, has unfortunately taken control. So argues Iain McGilchrist in *The Master and his Emissary,* his fascinating analysis of the delicate symbiosis between our head and our heart.

But each one of us needs both — logical thinking and intuitive timeless myths. Einstein, who felt a huge sense of wonder at the natural world, realized that science and art are two complementary ways of exploring the world — one objective, the other using the subjective subconscious. He knew the importance of creative thinking — it is how he discovered his world-changing scientific theories, in particular The Theory of Relativity. He was sitting in a tram on his way to work at the patent office one morning when he looked at the tram clock. 'What time would the clock show if the tram had the velocity of light?', he wondered. He was immersed in his subconscious. He called it 'possibility thinking', and it produced the most influential equation of all time: $E = Mc^2$. 'Imagination is more important than knowledge,' he said, 'for knowledge is limited, whereas imagination embraces the entire world, stimulating progress, giving birth to evolution.' His supporter in Relativity, the founder of Quantum Mechanics, Max Planck, also used the same 'what if' thinking process: 'Scientists must have a vivid intuitive imagination, for new ideas are not generated by deduction but by an artistically creative imagination.'

It was many years before Einstein's intuitive ideas were confirmed through scientific observation, and the same is true for Charles Darwin whose 'outside the box', as he called them, ideas led to the Theory of Evolution, which completely overthrew contemporary beliefs about the origin of the world, and when time began. 'I can remember the very spot in the road, whilst in my carriage, when to my joy the solution occurred to me,' Darwin wrote.

We need Logos and we need Mythos in our lives. Only then can we begin to understand time — *chronos* —

chronological time – and *kairos* – timeless time.

Yesterday evening, I told Francis I was writing a book called *A Timeless Moment,* dedicated to him. 'How wonderful,' he said. I asked, 'Do you remember you used that expression, Francis… what were you meaning… were you thinking of… T S Eliot's poetry? Or Proust perhaps?' 'No,' he said. 'I mean that you can't measure it.' My heart leaped. This was a glimpse into the old Francis.

But just as soon as he came back, he was gone again.

Spacetime

It's early morning (6. 41 am precisely by my chronological watch) and I have crept out of the camp-bed I sleep on, next to Francis's special bed, in which he is sleeping soundly. I look out from the window of my first-floor study directly above where Francis is sleeping, and peer through the sea mist to the large flat expanse of sea, calm this morning, and the endless shingle beach stretching to left and to right. These horizontals are intersected by a few vertical telegraph poles and in particular by the tallness of the Lookout tower slightly to my left. I see the curves of the staircase rail and the circles of the chimney pots. To my very far left, just out of sight, is a huge, beautiful, pure white sphere: It's Sizewell Nuclear Power Station, where the formula $E = Mc^2$ is in daily operation. And, because of this scientific equation we know that there is something else out there on the beach, an object which I can't see, which I have to imagine, just as Einstein did. An object called spacetime.

I try to visualise this object, this 'gravitational field', which is curved like an elastic sheet in space and time. Carlo Rovelli, whose book *The Order of Time* I have been grappling with, describes time as part of a complicated geometry woven together with the geometry of space. Spacetime has four dimensions, he says: height, depth, width and another, the invisible fourth dimension, time.

Rovelli tells us that because spacetime is made of the gravitational force which is all around us and is elastic, and curved or sometimes undulating, time is not absolute, but exists as part of this gravitational field. It is not an independent entity, it is relative. Not only its speed, but also its flow, its direction – the past, and the future.

To reach the innovative scientific conclusion of Relativity, Einstein, with his creative (artistic!) thinking combined the insights of Aristotle and Newton. For Aristotle, time is change, for Newton everything in the cosmos is connected. Einstein synthesized the breakthroughs of these two thinkers into spacetime; when and where are always located in relation to each other.

A swim along the littoral

As I swim along the littoral this morning time is slower for me than it was as I sat still upstairs at my computer, because at sea level I am physically closer to the gravitational mass of this planet, and I am moving. The closer I swim to the shoreline on a calm day like today, the more the gentle waves envelop me and carry me in their rhythm; and as I close my eyes I am again in a reverie inside my subconscious, in that place where creative thinking happens, which I call *zez*. The waves roll out and draw back in wavy lines as I wade through them to where my dressing gown is thrown on the pebbles; and the sea and the pebbles are elegant shades of taupe, still shrouded in mist.

Meanwhile, up at the top of the Lookout tower, time is flowing faster, as it is further from the Earth's mass. Hanging on the wall facing out towards the sea is *Littoral 1*. This sculpture, by Nigel Hall is formed (as is everything I now know) in spacetime, in four dimensions including the invisible dimension of time. Its shapes intertwine like the sea today, and its polished wood is almost a pale taupe. Nigel responds to time and to memories and to particular places, in this case the littoral, the changing shoreline, on Aldeburgh beach.

Change and uncertainty

The world is unpredictable, for it is ruled, Rovelli tells us, by the Uncertainty Principle, which is a key feature of Quantum Mechanics. And this morning, the day after yesterday, I am facing uncertainty, the wind – how fierce and unpredictable it is. I can see the gigantic waves and hear them crashing against the shore from my cosy home here. So I know that if I were to swim I would be spun around as if I were a garment in a washing machine, then bashed repeatedly against the shingle as I try to scramble out. So today I will walk along the littoral, beside this roaring sea, and think about time.

Time is change. This is the insight of Aristotle and of Einstein. In fact, everything in the universe is about change. Change feels like time. It is easy to understand that the sea is always changing – we can see it. But it's less obvious that each pebble, and indeed every single thing in life, alive or dead, is about ceaseless change.

Far from being inert, as Newton insisted, every single atom is dynamic. I pick up a pebble – if I were to look microscopically inside it, I would be amazed by the bizarre activity going on! Deep inside, matter – particles and antiparticles, called quanta, are governed by the Second Law of Thermodynamics, which triggers a network of events, each unpredictable and uncertain and which cause an increase in disorder!

If Carlo Rovelli had been keeping me company on my walk beside the sea, he might have pointed out that even the things that are most 'thing-like', pebbles for example, are nothing more than long events. 'The hardest stone', he says, 'is in reality a complex vibration of quantum fields, a momentary interaction of forces, a process that for a brief moment manages to keep its shape, to hold itself in equilibrium before disintegrating again into dust, a brief chapter in the history of interactions between the elements of the planet.'

Everything is a network of interactions – simple ones compounding into complex ones. So for example, Rovelli, pointing at a massive wave would have said: 'A wave is not a thing, it is a movement of water, and the water that forms it is always different.' A human being is, of course, the most complex series of events of all time, he could add, and these events increase disorder inside each and every atom inside us.

This increasing disorder caused by the Second Law of Thermodynamics, is called entropy and Rovelli explains it powers the cosmos. It powers change, the arrow of time.

The arrow points forward due to this increasing disorder, and also because the universe is expanding, says the late professor of cosmological physics, Stephen Hawking. And, he adds, we experience this flow internally, psychologically. We remember the past and anticipate the future. Change from low to high entropy is processed in our brain, with traces of previous low entropy being stored in our neurons as memory. These traces of memory are, Rovelli says, our blurred perception of previous states of lower entropy.

Here on Aldeburgh beach we (naturally) often listen to *Einstein on the Beach*, the minimalist opera by Philip Glass. The music is given meaning by the notes before and the notes after the present one. Thick time. Memory and anticipation. Silence. Glass counts out time - one, two, three, four.... Awareness of the passage of time is internal. But some centuries ago we would have been burnt at the stake for thinking this, for 'It is heretical to maintain that age and time do not exist in reality but only in the mind,' decreed The Bishop of Paris in 1277 in his *Condemnations*.

This morning the rhythm of the waves was perfect and I could close my eyes and *zez*, and think about Spinoza for whom God is inseparable from the laws of the universe, and for whom nature is the manifestation of God. This heretical point of view was thought in the middle of the seventeenth century long before anyone else dared think it, let alone speak it out loud. Baruch Spinoza not only studied mathematics, astronomy and physics, but also loved intuitive knowledge, flashes of insight, that suddenly fused all the information he had acquired from every source into a new vision, that he called 'beatitude'. He was imagining, *zezing*, as I do, and as Einstein (who identified closely with Spinoza) ensured he did, as easily as breathing; for our ability to switch easily and often between our conscious and subconscious minds is the *Homo sapiens* party trick. Imagination is somehow a vital human attribute; but to what purpose?

'I am certain… of the truth of imagination.' This is from another of Francis's favourite poets, the Romantic, John Keats, shortly before his death aged only 25. For his poetic insight an *ecstatic* attitude was essential, he was

'ready to plunge into the dark night of unknowing'. Insight occurs when 'a man is capable of being in uncertainties, mysteries, doubts, without any irritable reaching after fact and reason.'

Time? Change? Memory? Imagination? Consciousness? Creativity? Why? All this was whirring round in my subconscious as I closed my eyes while I swam this morning, the sea becoming a little choppy.

We know that our brain is made of the same star-stuff that makes up the universe. And just like the universe, our brains are programmed to maximize entropy, the increasing disorder going on all the time, every moment, in every cell in our body. Yet I, like every human being, feel the urge to make order, to take control. This is our daily struggle. We, said Stephen Hawking, create order out of disorder using energy. We are 'a small corner of order in a disordered universe,' he wrote. Why do we want to make order? is the question inside me as I *zez* as I swim.

Because making order is how we minimise the growing disorder of the universe. Making order is the creative urge which drives evolution, and it counters the negativity of entropy. Just as this thought surfaces into my brain, a huge wave crashes over my head and I swim furiously upwards through the swirling water to the air above, and then scramble out as fast as I can with another big wave chasing me, scolding myself for being immersed in my thoughts rather than noticing the increasingly rough sea, and I thank God for personally saving me from drowning. Inside the house, Francis is sitting in his special chair and he looks at me dripping wet and asks sweetly, as he does every morning, 'have you been swimming?'

Order and disorder

My mind is a still a swirl of order, disorder, change, memory, time, consciousness, imagination while the entirety of me - my mind and my body - is enveloped in a hot shower. Next, I'm back in pre-frontal cortex mode to do my emails. Then, next, I am submerged in my subconscious while I chop onions for risotto. The chopping job is an automatic rhythmic activity, like swimming, and allows the brain to revert into its default mode network, that altered state of consciousness which Einstein said we must enter for creative thinking, *zez*, to happen.

Back again into pre-frontal cortex to plan. The risotto is to be made into arancini, little balls of rice stuffed with lovely gooey mozzarella. We ate them in Venice doing a recce for our Venice Biennale project next year. But these little balls are fiddly and take ages, and I am getting anxious. I fear I am losing my struggle - disorder is winning over order. Why do I have this need to make them? Why don't I sit down quietly and read the newspaper? Because then I fear I would sink into increasing sloth. Creativity v Entropy. This is what life is about!

Sixty people are expected soon for our launch of *Einstein on Aldeburgh Beach*, and I realise that we don't have enough peach juice for the Bellinis. I do what humans do best. I improvise. In the cupboard I find a couple of tins of peaches and whizz them in an electrical gadget invented by a creative human helped by innovative collaborators. For, of course the *Homo sapiens* ability to turn our personal creativity into innovation is our supreme evolutionary niche. And those personal ideas become commodities which we barter or sell to make our livelihoods. 'It is the long history of mankind, those who have learnt to collaborate and improvise most effectively have prevailed,' said Darwin. We collaborate, our ideas, as eloquently phrased by the science thinker Matt Ridley, 'have sex' with the ideas of others. This cross-fertilisation of ideas is central to creativity, to innovation, to evolutionary adaptation.

Creativity must surely require consciousness to anticipate future needs and to remember useful things from past experience. Consciousness delivers memory and anticipation. **That** (I realise, in a flash of understanding) **is the reason why** *Homo sapiens* **are so successful at creatively adapting to evolutionary change – because we experience time through our possession of consciousness.** The peach juice is ready and we launch *Einstein on Aldeburgh Beach*.

Afterwards I do sit down to read the newspaper. But I'm still not concentrating, still thinking about entropy and creativity. I can't understand how these two opposing forces – one increasing disorder, the other increasing order, operate together inside one cell, ruled by quantum mechanics, and both fuelled by the sun.

Who can I ask? Yes! I know – Steve, my old friend Steve (he who coming down from the top of the Lookout cried out: 'From stardust to stardust!'). It is time for our 5 oclock cup of tea, which Francis and I drink as the clock simultaneously (as Einstein would say) strikes five. It is Saturday 9 June 2018, and the Queen's birthday honours are listed in *The Times*. Steve is now Sir Steven Cowley, knighted for services to science and nuclear fusion.

Steve (I must congratulate him) will surely know Professor Sir Roger Penrose, his fellow physicist based in Oxford. Sir Roger is convinced that the enigma of consciousness lies within the quantum mechanics of our neurons. He is seeking scientific evidence to support his intuition that a process akin to photosynthesis converts energy in microtubules inside our nerve cells, and this gives rise to consciousness.

I must work out what my question is…. evolution, creativity and consciousness must surely be one intertwined enigma? Together they are a process which conserves, transforms and focuses energy, which counters that other drive, entropy, which dissipates and disperses energy? Entropy, paradoxically, causes change which we experience as time, with its quality of memory, which our consciousness utilizes so it can, creatively, plan present and future evolutionary needs, so we can adapt to change, which is caused by entropy? The sun is the source of low entropy, and is also the source of energy!

I wanted, so desperately, that evening, to explore these ideas with Francis. But that sunny summer, when Steve and Margaret came, although I didn't know it, was the last time I could have.

Unpredictability and possibility

Yesterday morning the moon's gravitational pull had pushed the sea right out, but its powerful swells would have sucked me right in. So I walked along the surprisingly sandy beach which is revealed - a brand new littoral, and felt happy about the launch of *Einstein on Aldeburgh Beach*. The arancini were liked, but not worth the effort, and everyone drank the Bellinis, with my improvised peach juice. I did what humans do, which is to remember yesterday and anticipate the future. I thought of next year, when at the Venice Biennale we are presenting our next big idea – ALIVE in the UNIVERSE! Life and Death; Space and Time; Opposing forces and Myth and Logic make up our four-week art, science and philosophy marathon. It's all about the dichotomy of creativity and entropy! We must find out the answer!

This morning, after my swim, I am sitting in the sun in my favourite place, on our sheltered terrace overlooking the drama of the sea. I look all around me at this awesome world. Above me is a cacophony of seagull cries, and they are a chatty lot, talking to each other all the time. Heidegger thought about being and time, and decided that care is what being is all about. I disagree, Martin. Seagulls are way more caring than us humans. They pair for life. We watch them from our terrace selflessly nurturing their young for months, and then coping with the death of many or all of their chicks. They are clever and learn new ways of stealing food, but it is a predominantly learned instinct, because creativity is the human USP. No other animal is anywhere near us in this specialist department.

For it is our creativity which makes us human. So says D J Bronowski in *The Ascent of Man,* a book I find on Francis's shelf. As I look over the breath taking view of the roaring sea, I feel each human being has a life-enhancing role to play, to create in partnership with the universe, and we are each given the ability to do so each in our own unique way. I am reading Bronowski as I drink my juice on the terrace.

> It is our imaginative gifts, which distinguishes us from other animals: He makes plans, inventions, new discoveries, by putting different talents together and his discoveries become more subtle and penetrating, as he learns to combine his talents in more complex and intimate ways. So the great discoveries of different ages and different cultures, in technique, in science, in the arts, express in their progression a richer and more intricate conjunction of human faculties, an ascending trellis of his gifts.

How do we, *Homo sapiens* do this? Rovelli tells us that as with every atom in the universe, every cell of our sophisticated, clever brain is ruled by the unpredictable activity of quantum mechanics. This is why, I suggest, we *Homo sapiens* come up with the unpredictable, surprising and sometimes surprisingly wise creative solutions so vital for the success of the evolution of our species.

This is not, of course everyday prefrontal thinking (will my morning glass of juice be apple with mango or apple with orange?). This is the thinking we do for profound, life-changing, evolutionary challenges, when everyday thinking is stumped. What, for example, is the unique way that I can personally contribute to this world, and through it earn my livelihood? To do this, we look to solve mankind's problems, just as we did as early humans, when we found novel solutions to environmental challenges (the idea of a bridge, a wheel, a bone needle to sew animal skins). The *Homo sapiens* achievement is our success in adapting the environment to us and to adapting ourselves to the environment. And it was our brain's evolved capacity to think proactively (rather than simply reactively like all other animals) which was our forte, and the creative process emerged from our increasingly sophisticated brain, with its layers of consciousness, capable of choosing from self-generated alternatives.

I practise mindfulness, on the terrace; for a while enjoying my consciousness, being aware of the sun on my face, the sound of the sea, the screeching of gulls far away and near; and the taste on my lips of my apple with mango juice, bathed in the gentle buzzing of a wasp as he tries to drink it with me. 'Through our consciousness man gives the world its objective existence,' observed the Swiss psychologist Carl Jung.

We, *Homo sapiens,* have over time, gained enormous evolutionary advantage through consciousness with its unique quality of self-awareness. Creative thinking requires inventing brand-new combinations and this skill, the evolutionary biologist Nicholas Humphrey tells us, needs a sensitivity to similarity and difference, which humans gain through self-aware sensations called *qualia*. Self-awareness reveals itself as our conscious self, where we evaluate and realize ideas, and as our subconscious inner self, which we know as our soul, that reservoir from where we generate ideas.

It was the momentous evolutionary development of self-awareness that made us human, I propose. Our brain was already large, but around 75,000 years ago this cognitive advance caused a 'big bang' of cultural progress; and archaeologists have found evidence of tools used for hunting, cooking and living, as well as burial sites as we, at the same time, became aware of life and death.

Then I realize something. **The neural advancement of multi-layered human consciousness gave** *Homo sapiens* **the capacity to co-create, and thereby contribute, I suggest, in a more physics-efficient way to the creativity and evolution of the universe.** I define co--creation as the ability to harness energy from the universe and also from the conscious, subconscious and unconscious minds of all of humanity who has ever lived; then bathe it in the unique personality of our soul, and transform it into a new combination of energy waves – an idea, the brand new solution to our evolutionary challenge.

We do this through what I call *zez,* the mental equivalent of sex.

As I sit in the sunshine on the terrace, I am *zezing,* submerged in the alpha waves of my subconscious. The action is happening in my anterior superior temporal gyrus in the right hemisphere of my brain. Here my neurons have slightly longer dendrites capable of conducting impulses towards the cells, seeking out connections between my new challenge and the seemingly random thoughts of my subconscious. Like every one else, I have billions of bits of thoughts, observations, memories, feelings, floating around and each one presents a multitude of possibilities which evolve and change over time. Thoughts pop up and become entangled with other thoughts, influencing each other instantaneously, and then suddenly two neurons link, gamma rays spark! The idea rises up and surfaces into my conscious mind, like magic, and I shout 'yes!'

The awe of the everyday

Nimrod, from Transylvania, helps me get Francis up. Our new life involves a kind of intimacy that our romantic younger selves never envisioned. And for a once fiercely independent person, Francis has accepted his total dependence benignly. He would not be alive, nor would it be possible to manage his care well, without human creativity – for all human progress is the by-product of human creativity. Creativity is the ultimate source of all innovation and economic value – it touches every one of us every moment of every day, from our good health to our cup of cappuccino, and the concept of money to pay for it; to the flush toilet we sit on, to the safe streets we walk on. It enables Francis to see and chat to his far-away children and grandchildren in one click of the FaceTime icon. Without human creativity, I would have no children, for my triplets were created with the aid of IVF technology. We expect progress to continue onwards and upwards, but now we find some of our creative ideas have unintended negative consequences. Entropy fights back! For example, those 'good ideas' of refining carbohydrates and being socially connected through the internet makes our children fat and socially anxious. How much healthier it would be for them to be outdoors, playing imaginary games, thereby practising that part of the brain they will need as successful (ie creatively fulfilled) adults.

Einstein and Picasso: Revolutionaries in Space and Time. This is my brand new idea! Conceived on the terrace yesterday. Using outside-the-box creative thinking, both these men found complementary solutions, at exactly the same time (1905 -7) to exactly the same problem – how to understand space and time. Using visual imagery, Einstein came up with scientific solutions. Using geometry, Picasso came up with artistic solutions. And as I *zez* again, I feel euphoric as nature's reward, dopamine, squirts into my brain, as thoughts connect and more ideas come: Sir Roland Penrose was knighted for services to art – he was the major promoter of Picasso in the UK. His nephew, the Einstein medallist Sir Roger Penrose, knighted for services to science, is taking his fascination with the universe forward into the role of quantum mechanics in consciousness - which is so intertwined with creative thinking, the key ingredient of the success of the Penroses' double heroes, Picasso and Einstein.

Both Picasso and Einstein fought the Second Law of Thermodynamics, entropy, all their lives, as we all do. Both

Strawberry bosom pudding and cubist soup (as you place a spoonful in your mouth, its blending becomes the artwork) two course during his residency. Arts Club annual party. More arty parties in the Lookout. Francis and his old friend Willie Pryor sit in the rai

of many, served for our artists' feast conceived and cooked by the artist Lisa Adamczewski. The feast!! Lunch for Paul Kindersley

showed huge resilience through years of failure, rejection and poverty, before being hailed as geniuses. Their sense of identity was intimately bound up with the fragility of their self-belief. For inside our subconscious and unconscious minds, our psyche has embedded within it all sorts of thoughts, feelings and experiences, both good and bad. As part of the creative drive of the universe, our subconscious strives, through our creativity, to make order of this chaos. Einstein and Picasso each needed, as we all do, to be valued as a person with a unique expression to offer humanity, and expressing their creativity gave them that sense of control and self-esteem. For when creative energy lies dormant or is repressed, we feel a lack of control over our lives. This presents as anxiety, depression, self-harm and addiction. Expressed outwardly, we can be driven to seek fulfilment and a sense of belonging in the quickest, easiest and often only way open to us, through crime and violence. 'Terrorism is a failure to find creative solutions to life, to finding and fulfilling one's destiny,' writes Stephen A Diamond in *Anger, Madness and the Daimonic.*

Now it is evening. My watch reads 20.12pm precisely (*chronos* time), and Francis is in bed and I read to him the draft so far of *A Timeless Moment.* He likes it, he says. He and I are together in *kairos* time. I think about the way Francis expressed his unique creativity; how he transformed his creative energy into something to benefit humanity. His key skill was as the catalyst who helped others to bring their visionary ideas to fruition. He did this for all the many organizations for which he was trustee or chairman, and as he did as Sir Nicholas Serota's Deputy at Tate. Combining all his skills across a wide spectrum of life, Francis found himself one morning at the top of an old, disused power station overlooking the Thames in Southwark. He and a heritage-world contact looked down towards St Paul's and saw something visionary – that a bridge could connect it with the power station. The idea for Tate Modern could become reality in this derelict building in this potentially stunning location.

Now St Paul's and Tate Modern sit like spiritual twins in the heart of London, joined by their umbilical chord, the Millennium Bridge. Both are dominated by their gigantic central axis, the nave and the Turbine Hall, and both serve much the same purpose – to take people to that place they long for – *ekstasis*, when we step outside the humdrum of our daily life and enter the mystery of the universe. I went there a couple of months ago and was invited to participate at both, at St Paul's for morning Eucharist and at Tate Modern to swing on a triple swing, an art installation by the Danish collective, Superflex. I met a young artist friend at the top of the new Tate tower and as we looked across the river he said how obvious it is that St Paul's looks like a bosom with a nipple on top, and the chimney of Tate like a phallus. When I came home I asked Francis if he had thought this that first day. His answer was just as I was expecting.

Head and heart

Next morning, I creep out of my camp bed quietly and upstairs into the room which used to be Francis's study.

It's now my space of calm in a busy house because we have given over our beautiful bedroom on the top floor to Nimrod. This room's ensuite bathroom is where Francis lay on the floor for four hours. That evil bidet was punished and sat on the beach beside the Lookout all last year, given new use as a feminist's Duchampian urinal. In *Duchamp 100 Years Later* we marked a century since Duchamp presented a urinal as a work of art: 'It is art if I, the artist, say it is art.' This new thinking brought welcome change to the art world, no longer are artists constrained in how they express themselves. But Duchamp repressed his sexual feelings for his sister Suzanne, and needed to 'concentrate on converting my emotion into thought.' So conceptualism was born, with the idea more important than emotion. More head than heart.

I have kept Francis's room exactly as he left it, other than upgrading the old bathroom, and keeping my clothes and beautifying things in here. Francis had so many interests across a wide spectrum. I say 'had' because that part of his brain has, I fear, been destroyed by his subarachnoid haemorrhage. No longer is he interested, curious, creative. Yet the hundreds of books on his shelves bear witness to the richness of the life he lived, which interwove into his personal creativity. Here are rows of poetry books; as an adolescent he learned a poem a day, a repertoire which he could, until his accident, recite precisely, on request. But not now. Interestingly, the snatches of poetry that come from somewhere within, sometimes when I ask, are invariably by T S Eliot.

Here are shelves of piano music scores and old records, cassettes and CDs. I found the Bible given to Francis by his prep school headmaster, with its personal inscription to him:

> Be strong and of good courage:
> Be not afraid, neither be thou dismayed.
> The Lord thy God is with thee
> Whithersoever thou goest.

And books on every religion, many delved into by us together, a few years ago, when I dragged him round to every place of worship on offer in London – the Mormon Church, the Pentecostal, the Baptist, a synagogue, the Greek Orthodox, the Church of Scientology.

There are books on wild flowers, on our planet, on every single subject because he wanted to know about everything. But he loved to read, for his own enjoyment more than anything, adventure books. There are rows of John Buchans, and more recently every Anthony Horowitz. But then that beautiful mind stopped being inquisitive, in a split second.

Francis Carnwath left his prep school with an Oppidan Scholarship to Eton, a dashing (in my opinion) member of Pop. Then Trinity College, Cambridge. He followed his father into merchant banking, at Barings, but left five years before its devastating collapse, fearing its reckless banking attitude would get it into trouble. Then began

The view from Francis's room

his personal drive for independence – Tate; The Heritage Lottery Fund; The Royal Naval College, Greenwich. And his very many voluntary responsibilities: Shelter; Spitalfields; The Darwin Trust; The Blue Plaques (as Chairman he unveiled something like 97 blue plaques over ten years in London); The Outsider Trust; the Musicians Society; The Yorkshire Sculpture Park; Thames 21. His pragmatic intelligence, natural charm, lack of ego, and extraordinarily extensive network of friends and contacts in high places made him an ideal chairman. He was tireless and quietly driven; I ask him: 'By what?' And he says with his usual self- deprecation, 'Just carrying on.'

Francis would support his friends and family by buying their memoirs (he planned one day to write his own, on how bureaucracy tries to stop new things happening.) I read many of them, from the homely to the truly enlightening and in each the author is, ultimately, as we all are, grappling to understand the meaning of life. The paintings he collected from artist friends hang on the walls; and every surface is covered with little bowls full of paperclips and stamps and biros, now dry. Photographs are propped up, some now curled and faded, of his three beautiful children, two daughters and a son, playing in the garden of the old rectory, the family home. And some, more obviously recent and colourful, are of his sweet grandchildren. Some are of me and some are of him and me. I find, on a bottom shelf, an old album which falls apart as I open its thick, black cartridge pages dotted with miniscule black and white photos of a young Francis from an earlier era, with his five younger siblings, bathing on Dunwich beach a few miles from here. And tucked, modestly, into the back of one such album is a smiling Francis from a few years ago, receiving his CBE.

I pick out books and bring them down so Francis and I can read and re-read them together. Each book has memories. I don't choose *Annie's Box*, for it is weighted with the sadness Francis was feeling when I first met him. Like Darwin, Francis was full of incomprehension and grief at the death of one of those beautiful daughters, who was just a few years younger than Darwin's daughter, Annie, when she died. 'The Lord thy God', no longer seemed to be with Francis 'whithersoever' he went, and it was this that helped turn Francis into the questioner that he became, so that I found pamphlets by doubting men of the church like the Bishop, John Robinson, on his shelves.   I choose contrasting books and read bits of them to him alternately, one on cosmology with one on religion, for example.

Transformation

I learn a bit more about physics from some old pamphlets on his shelf, and am intrigued.   The new book by Carlo Rovelli explains the Second Law of Thermodynamics – increasing disorder (called entropy) and my curiosity now wants to know what the First Law of Thermodynamics is.   Easiest just to Google.   It is 'a law of conservation of energy which states that the total energy of an isolated system is constant; energy can be transformed from one form to another, but can be neither created nor destroyed.'

My study with sculpture by Henry Piper

Fun on the beach (clockwise from bottom left)

Lunch in the rain on the terrace. CW, Joan Edlis, Sam Gordon Clark, Francis, Jane Gordon Clark. Why is Francis wearing black
performance. The Three Pianists play for Frances: Peter Dickinson, Humphrey Burton and Roger Wright. The very first gatherin
of brand new, but discarded, shopping bags retrieved from rubbish bins around Mayfair as a beach sculpture. My assistant, Cand
cloth from the Lookout into the sea, an art work by Susan Brinkhurst. Paul Boucher, Melvyn Tan and Heather Newill look wistfu
urinal. Thomas Ades one Aldeburgh Festival came to say hello.

n the beach talking to the artist Clara Drummond? A performance work by Declan Jenkins. Mark Fuller with sculpture in mid
e Lookout includes Alan Britten, Christina and Humphrey Burton and Mary Allen. Catherine Shakespeare Lane installs hundreds
ockett, with members of Francis's family and my family all mucking in together eating fish and chips on the beach. Embroidered
culprit, the green hand of the artist Declan Jenkins. The evil bidet punished with a year on the beach as a feminists' Duchampian

It's what causes pistons to go up and down so that engines move forward, Google says.

Next morning, I look at the little bathroom that used to be Francis's and the room which was his study. My mess is everywhere and I am in despair. I go for a swim with thoughts swirling in my brain. Afterwards, as I take my time to have a shower and wash my hair it becomes obvious. **To conserve energy most efficiently, as required by the First Law of Thermodynamics, energy is transformed in a process which (perhaps only as consequence) generates creativity and evolution.** The clue is the word 'transform' for this is what we do when we create: we transform one form of energy into another, from the nutritious food we eat into creative ideas (just as when heat is applied, gas is transformed into kinetic energy which drives the engine.) Is it The First Law of Thermodynamics, then, which drives us to make order out of disorder? For we are programmed, I read, by physics, to minimize the growth of unusable energy in an isolated system, which is the universe. Here is the twentieth-century evolutionary biologist, Sir Julian Huxley's definition of evolution:

> Evolution in the extended sense can be defined as a directional and essentially irreversible process occurring in time, which in its course gives rise to an increase of variety and an increasingly high level of organisation in its products. Our present knowledge indeed forces us to the view that the whole of reality is evolution – a single process of transformation.

It became clear to me, in the shower. **We have two opposing drives competing inside us: The First Law of Thermodynamics which (in order to conserve energy, ie stop it becoming unusable) generates order - resulting in the intertwined processes of creativity and evolution; and the Second Law which causes disorder (entropy) as energy becomes increasingly unusable. And we experience these conflicting laws internally, just as we experience time (change) internally. All our thoughts and actions are but reactions to these two fundamental, interacting, conflicting processes. This internal conflict of physics is the daily challenge we each feel. And to counter the relentlessness of entropy, of disorder, we are programmed to make order, which is our creativity, and this is how we** *Homo sapiens* **contribute (so successfully) to evolutionary adaptation.**

Dressed now, I fish out a book by Matt Ridley I read a couple of years ago. In *The Evolution of Everything* he explores how we have underestimated the power of spontaneous, organic and constructive change driven from below - in culture, economics, technology, education – indeed in everything. Yes, we have – and this power, the general theory of evolution (as he calls it) is, I suggest, the First Law of Thermodynamics. Creativity is the niche of *Homo sapiens* in the universe, for as Einstein said 'Imagination embraces the entire world, stimulating progress, giving birth to evolution.' And we all 'just carry on' as Francis would say, in our struggle to win in this game of thermodynamics.

'It is not the strongest of the species that survive nor the most intelligent, but the ones most responsive to change.' Darwin's insight goes to the heart of physics. Likewise, Stephen Hawking identifies intelligence as our ability to adapt to change. The continuous interactions happening inside all animate and inanimate things – just as Rovelli was saying – cause incessant change, and the business of life, for *Homo sapiens*, is, I suggest, to respond to that change most efficiently, using creativity as our tool.

My messy room is entropy, increasing disorder, leading, if I leave it, to total decay. I must use the First Law and apply my energy (my 'work') to put order into this room. I am transforming energy from the sun (photosynthesized into my breakfast of muesli with yoghurt) into another form of energy – kinetic – which I use to clean. I enlist the co-operation of other creative humans to make my energy transfer more efficient by using a Dyson vacuum cleaner, and by squirting Co-op cleaning fluid around the basin. While I do this I am *zezing*, transforming energy from the sun into new ideas (like my new idea of *Einstein and Picasso: Revolutionaries in Space and Time*, and this book, *A Timeless Moment*, and ALIVE in the UNIVERSE for the Venice Biennale – for all of them are incubating in my subconscious.) Just as someone else has transformed their unique creative energy into their brilliant idea of the hairdryer to help me bring order to my hair, still wet and unruly from my shower.

The wonder of why

Next day, sunny and hot but very windy, Francis and I are on the seafront trying unsuccessfully to hold on to the newspapers and realizing why. The why of everything in life becomes clear. It is **because of that struggle between the First and the Second Laws of Thermodynamics**. And because we are, each of us, 'open systems'. In thermodynamics, I read, a closed (or isolated) system might be the universe in that no energy or matter can enter or leave. Within that system we, and everything else, are open, and for example, we, humans, take in energy from the sun as heat, and as (delicious, that lunchtime – Dover sole straight from the fisherman) food, and we excrete unusable energy as heat and sweat and matter as waste (we go to the toilet).

In addition to our physical requirement for thermodynamic tension which keeps us striving as living organisms, we each have our own personal mental struggle, our striving for the perfect mental slight dis-equilibrium. Amazingly, every single news item from politics, to inequality, social sciences, economics, education, sport, racism, to social gossip is a graphic twenty-first-century description of the human race's self-perpetuating mental struggle to reach a compromise between the First and Second Laws of Thermodynamics.

And tragically everywhere in the newspapers is war. Why is there war? Why bloody wars over the most trivial of religious dogma? Now we know. Because the Laws of Thermodynamics require each of us to be part of an efficient energy-conserving/transforming cluster, and these self-help groups compete with each other to be top dog in the law of evolution. If we *Homo sapiens* are not efficient and not responsible, another animal species is vying to take over our prime spot on the evolutionary ladder, maybe those wily competitors of ours – rats,

The lady in the Tower, photograph by the artist Bill Jackson, 2014

cockroaches or seagulls.

Francis and I love listening to BBC radio 4 early on Sunday mornings when it invariably delivers a big dose of thermodynamic human drama. The World Service reports on the saga of worldwide atrocities (on-going human insecurity as we struggle between these two laws of physics). Then my favourite *Something Understood*, when Mark Tully takes an abstract issue like love, and explores it through spirituality, poetry, prose and music. Then a most depressing programme, *Sunday*, about the on going political infighting of religion (the two Laws doing overtime).

Perfection

Now it's just gone 8 o'clock on Sunday morning and I am in Francis's old study looking out at the sea. How 'far-fetched' are those waves, I am wondering. Then, next moment, I am in ecstasy! I hear the rousing hymns of *Sunday Worship*… but then, too soon, too brutally, I am jolted out of it: 'You therefore must be perfect, as your heavenly Father is perfect'. These stern words come from the old radio on Francis's desk. I look despairingly at a huge pile of disorder - sheets to be ironed - and get out a couple of manifestations of human creativity, an ironing board and an iron, both of which enable me more efficiently to apply my energy to make order out of this disorder.

Ironing is a repetitive action (like swimming) which induces the brain to enter its default mode network, ideal for creative thinking. So as I iron, I am inside my subconscious, but also vaguely listening to that vicar on the radio telling me that I must repent of my sins. I must try to be perfect, he says. This reminds me of something I have just read. Between ironing duvet covers, I take *A Brief History of Time* off the shelf and find the page. At the beginning of time, Stephen Hawking writes, the universe was regular and smooth, but then it became more and more lumpy and disordered over time. Yes of course – this is it! **Could religion be our internal intuition so we understand subliminally the laws of physics?** We feel these laws inside us, just as we feel time inside us. This is why, I suggest, we remember (through the collective unconscious) the perfection of the beginning of time, the story of the Garden of Eden. We look forward to perfection at the end of time, to timelessness, when we are free from the relentless demand of time, the conflict between the two Laws of Thermodynamics, between creativity and entropy, order and disorder.

Creativity, it feels to me, encourages positive action which assists the evolutionary success of our species. Entropy feels negative, and because of it, we sin. We sin because of our feelings of insecurity, our fear of failure. We feel despair and anxiety as we are overwhelmed by the continuing disorder of life, and our bad action or inaction is the consequence.

This struggle is caused by the pressure of time and we dream of timelessness, of eternity, of heaven, nirvana, paradise, salvation when we will be released from this dilemma.

'God' is timeless and perfect. He (!) is also love, I am told repeatedly by the vicar on the radio. Love, yes, could this be physics' beautiful and effective bonding agent? Perhaps because each of us is an 'open system' we need the support (delivered as love) of those fellow human beings in our (as physicists call it) 'surroundings', in our personal cluster, to help make our energy usable in the most efficient way. We want to support those in thermodynamic sympathy with us, but not others; that's why we have wars. We have compassion for those in our 'surroundings', for if their energy becomes less usable, it affects the efficiency of our personal cluster. Unusable energy builds up as high entropy, heat death, which we call hell, where we are all destined unless we repent of our sins, as the vicar says.

All the ironing is done, and I feel satisfying squirts of dopamine into my brain as reward for making some small order in this increasingly disordered system. Now I am swimming and I float with the rhythm of the waves, but also aware of life's uncertainty. I am thinking about the Uncertainty Principle and how it rules the quantum dynamics of each of our cells in our body. We crave certainty. That is what religions offer! Today I was offered certainty, a guaranteed place in heaven if I come to God through 'His son' Jesus Christ. Certainty! Timelessness guaranteed. The thought comforts me in my thermodynamic struggle.

Eternal damnation

Francis and I have both failed the test. He answered two maybes and one no, and I answered two nos and one maybe. This test is set us by Lord (Richard) Harries, former Bishop of Oxford, and you can find it on YouTube. It is called *3 Things Christians Must Believe:*
1) The Incarnation of Jesus Christ
2) The Resurrection of Jesus Christ
3) The Afterlife.

So Francis and I are officially not Christians. I had long thought this about myself; but not Francis – he had thought, that as he was brought up a Christian and has led a good, caring and neighbourly life, that he could count himself as one. But no, unfortunately, we may well both be on our way to eternal damnation (heat death, hell). Not because we are sinners, but because we didn't answer those three questions 'correctly'. We are ousted out of the Christian thermodynamic cluster.

Reader, you may (possibly) wonder why I spend so much time thinking about this subject. The answer is that, like all of us, I am spurred on to action through emotion. In 1975, on my solo journey round India, I volunteered for a

The drawing room with pictures (L-R) by Tessa Newcomb, Tai Shan Schierenberg, Patrick Heron, Grenville Davey, Rachel Nichols

1 Goss. Sculpture on table by Roger Hardy.

couple of weeks for the Missionaries of Charity in Calcutta. It was an uplifting experience helping the Sisters of Mercy as they selflessly cared for the sick and dying. On the Sunday I joined them for the weekly service held, as I remember, in a small home-made chapel somewhere in the hospital. As a convent girl, I had been confirmed and was not expecting to be tapped on the shoulder and excluded from taking holy communion. Very upset, I asked to see Mother Teresa to ask her why this should be. I was taken to the Mother House, to her study. She was genuinely understanding but explained that while she personally believed Protestant Christians, like me, should be allowed to receive the sacrament in a Catholic place of worship, she feared the Papacy would not change its rules.

I can, over 40 years later, still feel the hurt of that experience. Perhaps it marked the beginning of my personal E M Forster quest.

I had gone, a few evenings before Francis and I took our Christianity test, to the Royal Academy in London where a leading artist, the sculptor Sir Antony Gormley, discussed the relationship between the Christian tradition and contemporary visual art with a leading theologian, Lord (Rowan) Williams, former Archbishop of Canterbury. There was much smiling and head-nodding as they talked.

Afterwards, I asked an elderly gentleman with a red shirt and dog collar what he thought of the discussion. This kindly-looking man was (he introduced himself) Lord (Richard) Harries. Luckily, I had read this former Bishop of Oxford's book *GOD outside the box* with Francis a few years ago, so I asked him the question I had formulated in my mind during the evening's discussion: 'Do you think religion and the arts are both ways through which we strive to feel a sense of transcendence, a way to reach timelessness, of perfection which we may call God, or heaven, or paradise or nirvana or salvation?' It was as though I had touched him with a hot poker, 'No!', he choked. 'Christianity is a revealed faith; it is through Jesus Christ that we come to God, they are NOT ways to the same place.'

This encounter is why I Googled Lord Harries and found his Christianity test on YouTube. He also says, in *3 Things Christians must believe*, that it is fundamental to Christianity that we believe that God is a just judge, for there must ultimately be, he says, some kind of reconciliation and resolution.

The day of judgement. Help!

It reminds me of the little ditty which Francis still remembers by heart:

> The rain it falleth everyday
> Upon the just and unjust fella
> But mostly on the just because
> The unjust has the just's umbrella.

Time present and time past

It takes all my courage to go for a walk along the river Alde, because this is what Francis and I used to do in the afternoons, whenever we could. It has been three and half years now. I knew his absence would dominate. I miss his urbanity. I miss his knowledge of the seabirds, of every wild flower, of every tree. I miss his descriptions of the hilarious ways animals and insects reproduce. I am not, on this walk, as I was then, enchanted with poetry, or entertained by daft limericks, each precisely relevant to the particular moment.

So while I walked I thought about then, my memories. Now. The future.

'I can see the past, present and future, existing all at once. Before me.' William Blake had it just right.

For where are those afternoons Francis and I walked together? I am in search of lost time. Are they stored in a cosmic filing cabinet? Do they exist now? Did they exist then, but not now? Perhaps they only existed the moment they happened. Only my memory of them remains. And change.

If Francis could have been with me he might well have recited T S Eliot:

> Time present and time past
> Are both perhaps present in time future
> And time future contained in time past.

As I walk on I sing to myself this beautiful song by Sandy Denny. She had a beautiful voice; her own time was too short:

> Across the purple sky, all the birds are leaving
> But how can they know it's time for them to go?
> Before the winter fire, I will still be dreaming
> I have no thought of time
>
> For who knows where the time goes?
> Who knows where the time goes?

Back home Francis and I share a peach.

> Do I dare to eat a peach?
> I shall wear white flannel trousers, and walk upon the beach.

I have heard the mermaids singing, each to each.

I do not think that they will sing to me.

Yesterday we also ate a peach. I remember. There is a record of it because there was only one peach on the plate today, while yesterday there were two. The only record of yesterday is my memory and change (ie one peach less). So I am persuaded that time as an independent entity does not exist, but we feel it because of the physics of change happening within us and the world around us.

Plato warns us, through his parable of the cave, that reality is not as it seems, don't take it at face value. So, we must ask ourselves, is this world of time real? Timelessness, the eternal image of forms, is, for Plato, more real than this life where we experience time. Maybe the universe beyond is timeless, where we are no longer subject to the physics we experience as time? This may be why we, within this universe, this closed physics system, where we experience positive and negative changes as time, yearn for something beyond this time prison. **That something may be timelessness; which some people describe as God.** This would explain why the three Abrahamic religions insist that God is separate to his creation. Because timelessness (God) is outside our closed system, the universe, God's creation.

The nowness of now

Next morning is beautifully fresh – the joy of being here is that every day is always different, always very. Very blowy, very rainy, very sunny, very misty. All day it seems we have visitors – friends, artists, for Aldeburgh is a cultural meeting place, and we are right on the sea-front.

That evening I want to discuss Now with Francis. Has Now been the same throughout time, or does it change? Is Now not always the same, but also always different and transformed? As long as Now is consecutive and successive, it is different. Is Now part of the past and also of the future? If Now changes constantly, the previous Now needs to be stopped for replacing the current Now. But this can't happen in the same time as the current Now exists.

Aristotle, 2500 years ago thought all this, and continued:

> If Now constantly transforms, if no part of time being different are not concurrent (unless the part it involves and the part involved is involved by as some shorter time being involved by longer time) and if Now which is not (existing previously), it should have been stopped at a time, thus the Nows cannot be concurrent together rather the previous Now must have been stopped for being. However, the previous Now cannot have been stopped on their own (because in that case they need to have been existed) and it cannot be in the other Now. Therefore, we

might assume the Now cannot be in side with the other unless momentarily. Thus, if the Now cannot sit with the other Now, in that case it is imperative for numerous Nows to exist together….

…and so on.

Francis and I are trying to get our heads round Aristotle's thoughts on time and Nowness, but not easy. Eight hundred years ago, Saint Thomas Aquinas also had a go and asked: 'When something is comprised of parts and components which do not exist, how can that thing contribute to reality?'

We are mentally exhausted.

My triplet sons, now grown men, and their girlfriends come to stay for a (very) rainy, (very) windy weekend, and we talk about their careers; how (I ask) are they transforming their unique creativity into something to benefit humanity? Each is, in his very different way, they say. None is, thank goodness, in a rut, and this is the test. If you feel in a rut then you are not expressing your unique creativity fully, I say. Its been a full-on weekend of cooking, eating, drinking and chatting, and a break from thinking about time and timelessness. But when they leave I am back to it. The former Bishop, Lord Harries, when I mentioned timelessness that evening after the RA talk, recited lines from T S Eliot. No doubt he was sure of his position (about Jesus being the only way to 'God') because he knew that T S Eliot (the author of the sublime 'timeless' poetry Francis and his generation quote) had converted to Anglo Catholicism. Why would Eliot do that, I wonder?

Fear and guilt

But I am sure of my position too. Later that evening I was cleaning the kitchen and complaining to the former Bishop, in my mind, that the Christian church today does not seem to have moved on from 500 years ago when everyday life was dominated by religion and superstition. That's when Martin Luther lived, and he suffered terribly from the effects of entropy – he was anxious and depressed, and was petrified of going to hell, even though he was a model monk. The Bible is full of eschatological (Second Law of Thermodynamics) end-of-time fears of death, judgement and the final destiny of the soul and of humankind. Luther wanted to know that he was definitely saved, and so he invented Justification (salvation) through Faith Alone. Certainty!

And another thing, Bishop. As well as fear of damnation, guilt is another problem Christians suffer. This originates from another man who suffered terribly from the negative effects of entropy. Yes, you guessed, Augustine. This saint was distressed that he was unable to control his penis, and became obsessed with the idea that Adam's sin was within him, and in each of us, through sexual transmission from our common ancestor, Eve. He did, however, think about time:

Two moments in time, 25 years apart. Left to right (in each photo) - Hugo, Max and Gus.

It is within my mind, then, that I measure time. I must not allow my mind to insist that time is something objective. When I measure time, I am measuring something in the present of my mind. Either this is time, or I have no idea what time is.

But I am cross with him for displacing his sexual guilt on to billions of innocent people around the world over centuries through his invention of the notion of original sin, which is only redeemed through faith in the 'new Adam', ie Jesus Christ, the symbol of perfection. For political reasons the church accepted this grotesque doctrine just as it did Justification through Faith Alone, for the same ungodly reason. It also gave sanction to the tradition of interpreting the Bible, not as metaphorical timeless myth, as it had always been, but as literal truth – as you seem inclined to do, if I may say so, Bishop.

The kitchen is clean. It's very late, and I am dying to go to bed, but I am upstairs looking through Francis's Qur'an (a present from me). It is not unlike the Bible, but with fewer good stories and less violence. Like the Bible, but with more repetition, it directs us to do what we are told. Using non-physics language, it orders us to follow the two Laws of Thermodynamics, with the threat of fear and guilt, as Christianity does. Paradise, our reward, is described as 'gardens, with rivers flowing beneath', where those who enter will be greeted by angels, with words of peace, ie the perfection of the universe without those annoying laws of physics, without time. Hell, on the other hand, is the punishment where those who have failed go, and it is 'hell-fire' and chaos (entropy) because those 'sinners' have not obeyed the two laws of physics.

It seems a tragedy, to me, that the beautiful spirituality at the heart of most religions has been ruined by unhelpful dogma. Religion, as E M Forster accepted, can provide its followers with 'tenderness, pity and love' but it is 'conditional on certain beliefs and behaviours'. Carrot and stick. We see this in the Christian church, and I read in a Sunday supplement today, the story of a young Muslim, Ali al-Durrani. Al-Durrani was (like St Augustine) full of guilt about his teenage desires, and he hated being a sinner and craved redemption. He was hugely influenced by the father of modern jihad, the Egyptian radical, Sayyid Qutb. But Qutb was another man possessed with a bad case of entropy and was petrified of women and anything western, and he inflicted this negativity upon many young Muslims, who went on to join Al Qaeda and ISIS.

But I am pleased to say that now, the Sunday supplement says, Aimen Dean, as al-Durrani is now called, has renounced jihad.

It's even later now (12.15 am) but just one (last!) thought, as Francis is sleeping (I can hear him from up here, snoring hard). Just as Francis was uncomprehending of the death of his young daughter (as was I at the death of my own long- awaited baby, Victoria) so Christians have long been aware that it is difficult to explain why God allows human suffering. This is the subject of another book, an exquisite little one, I found on Francis's shelf, by C S Lewis, and which I am looking at now. Lewis loved stories, and as a little girl I wanted so much to believe in his fantasy world of Narnia. Lewis, like Bishop Harries, wants us grown-ups to believe in the complete Christian story with its virgin birth and resurrection. He attributes the feeling of the numinous, or awe as he calls it, together with our sense of morality, as being a good argument for the existence of God, a wise and good Creator and preferable to a universe ruled by chance and indifference. He discusses divine omnipotence and goodness, human wickedness, hell and heaven.   In fact C S Lewis's book is a textbook on the two Laws of Thermodynamics, but called by different names. We are made 'perfect' through suffering, he says.

Perfection is the goal, it seems to me, of both physics and theology.

I'm going to bed.

A journey in time

This morning the high tide washes me up on the littoral, on the shingle bank, and I sit for a while letting the swash and backwash run over me, back and forth. And there facing me are hundreds, thousands, millions, billions of pebbles - as many as there are stars in the sky - all carefully sorted by the sea, by size, into neat rows! They all seem, at first glance to look much the same, but like each human being, each one is unique. Each has its own personal history, and may have travelled just a few or many, many thousands of miles from all sorts of exotic or less exotic beginnings. Each is also journeying in time, transforming from fragment of rock to grain of sand over anything from 60 to 120 million years. Inside each we see a fascinating combination and pattern of chemical compounds including, in some cases crunched-up microscopic fossilised sea creatures. And microscopically inside each one, as we know from Rovelli, is a dynamic world of vibrating quantum fields. I invite holiday-makers, as they look with wonderment at our fairy tale tower (we once staged Rapunzel in it) to consider the purpose of existence and write it in a few words on a pebble as part of our project *Pebble Homage*. This is very popular, especially with families, and pebbles are piled in an installation around the tower, and become gradually scattered around the beach to be found, maybe, by future generations. Here's one I picked up as I walked past the table on which they are newly piled from yesterday:

>We are all individuals, like the stones on the beach. We reach for the stars, but they're all out of reach!

I've had several days for the thoughts of C S Lewis to immerse themselves in my subconscious. His words, I realize, are the key to understanding life. But, then, as I walk in the front door to our house from the beach, I suddenly remember the potato wedges in the top oven of the Aga, from last Sunday's lunch! When triplets and girlfriends were here. While I retrieve the hot oven tray with its black bits of entropied potato well on their way to charcoaled decay and death and soak the pan, I think about C S Lewis. Like other theologians, he encourages us to choose the 'perfect' God rather than our selfish selves, and take 'Him' into our lives. But this is exactly **what**

Maggi Hambling with David Remfrey RA. Richard Demarco "New beginnings are in the offing!" Maggi Hambling launching the mo...
Eileen's studio. Art dealer Sam Fogg, Francis, artist Marilyn Baiiley and art dealer Rene Gimpel. Artists Perienne Christian and Ryan G...
An artistic conversation includes the curator Cedar Lewisohn, art historian Martin Gayford, broadcaster Razia Iqbal and art critic Si...
Phillip King with Cedar Lewisohn. Two Royal Academians: Spencer de Grey and Chris Orr.

h on Margaret Mellis by Andrew Lambirth, our first ever event in the Lookout. Eileen Cooper RA with CW, the Lookout has become
Francis's beloved piano was prepared for a John Cage recital by John Snijders, listened to by artists Sue Arrowsmith and Ian Davenport.
Wilson. Tate curator Judy Collins. Alison Wilding RA with her dealer, the late Karsten Schubert. Past president of the Royal Academy,

Nina and her mistress, Tessa Newcomb, pose for the camera.

we do when we choose to transform our unique creative energy into something to benefit humanity. This is how we participate in one creative universe; how we contribute our unique selves, in a 'physics-efficient' way, to this project called life. We are part of a whole, which we call the universe, as Einstein said. This giving of ourselves to the whole brings forth a feeling of transcendence, a hint of timelessness, a timeless moment. Participating in this cosmic mystery, for me, is finding God.

A friend is right to query, "a timeless moment must surely be a contradiction?" Yes, he is right, and yet he is also not right. It is a paradox, as T S Eliot was the first to admit.

In the shower I have a further thought for the former Bishop, Lord Harries. The word 'love' is used by Christians to describe 'the unknowable' God. But love and belongingness are virtues which most naturally arise when we find our personal equilibrium, our purpose in life, when we fall in love with the universe. Moral decay, Bishop, is not, I feel sure, the inevitable consequence of religious decline; we can lead exemplary lives as individuals outside, in the world of independent, free thinking, in a society such as our own which values laws and morals, and where we can take moral responsibility for our own lives. For the personal expression of our unique creativity, in all its extraordinary, surprising and life-affirming ways empowers us with love and gratitude to give back to the world. For you know that religion demands a humility before the divine Creator, humility which has little room for independence. This is why the Christian church isn't that keen on independent thinking, or on the comments of artists (your colleague, Lord Williams, you may remember, hinted at this during the RA talk).

Richard Holloway, who was, as you know, a fellow Bishop of yours, reflects on life and death in his sensitive and sensible book *Waiting for the Last Bus* (you may have read it?). 'The riddle', Richard Holloway writes, 'is that without having any meaning itself, the universe generated human creatures with a need for meaning, who then projected meaning onto its speechless blankness. They thought it had spoken to them, had disclosed itself. But it was their own words they were hearing, their own longing they were fulfilling. It was all in the mind, the human mind, the only mind the universe possesses. That is an answer that hurts me. Because I think it may be right.'

Another thing, I think, while getting dressed – the world's totalitarian regimes, religious as well as nationalistic, hate independent thinking. But if we are not dominated by afterlife anguish we can think freely and creatively and devote our singular talents to making this incredible life here on earth its very best for humankind.

The thinker Yuval Noah Harari advocates that we, as liberal humanists, can draw from our inner experiences, to give meaning to our lives and to give meaning to the universe. I am still thinking about this as I get ready for bed; for, to counter this humanism, Francis has queried - what about the presence he and many people experience of a personal God who we feel is close to us? I prepare my suggestion for him... Through prayer, or meditation or creative thinking (*zezing*), we connect with the collective unconscious and are nourished by the souls of everyone who has ever lived and will ever live. The collective soul becomes the universal soul becomes the personal universe, becomes (for some) the personal God.

Celebrity visitors to the Aldeburgh Beach Lookout and ArtHouse (bottom left clockwise)

Diana Quick. A raucous Arts Club lunch. Liz Calder. Simon Schama and Mary Nighy, with her mother Diana Quick looking in the w
Eleanor Mills and Rachel Johnson. Jill Green and Anthony Horowitz in front of a Terry Frost painting. Late at night taking a sneak loo

a work by Eileen Haring Woods). Humphrey Burton and Joan Bakewell at the top of the Lookout. Michael Gambon. Ed Victor with e stunning installation by Issam Kourbaj at the top of the Lookout: Alan Yentob, Vanessa Branson, CW, Nicola Green.

Alleluia

> Alleluia! Sing to Jesus;
> His the sceptre, His the throne.
> Alleluia! His the triumph…,

Next morning, we are listening on the radio to the morning service and we sing together, now rather feebly, for gone are the days when Francis would belt out hymns. Tears stream down my face – how beautiful is the love of humankind, and I realize, emotionally, why it was that T S Eliot wanted to be a Christian:

> …His the victory alone.
> Hark! The sound of peaceful Zion
> Thunder like a mighty flood;
> Jesus out of ev'ry nation
> Has redeemed us by His blood.

I ask Francis what he thinks of my proposition that we human beings are ruled internally by the two laws of thermodynamics. 'OK', he says, 'but its not very romantic.'

That afternoon I spread Francis's many books on religion all around us. And we find something extraordinary – all of the ancient religions are an expression of human intuition for the laws of physics; all things good (First Law of Thermodynamics) and all things bad (Second Law). They look forward to perfection at the end of time.

Here is Zoroaster writing in about 1000 BC:

> I recognized you, Mazda Ahura, as holy and divine. I saw you as the
> Beginning and the Everlasting when life began. At that time you
> Commanded a reward for thoughts, words and deeds that are good,
> And you ordained through your wisdom that the wicked will receive
> An evil consequence, and that the good will receive the consequence
> Of their goodness. So it will be until the end of time.

Here, for example, is an old Hindu verse, referring to Brahman and *atman* (his presence in humans).

> Know the One alone, the Self, from whom are woven heaven, earth
> And space, as also the mind and all the vital breaths. Abandon
> Whatever else is said: this is the bridge to Immortality.

The Rig Veda hypothesizes that Timelessness is God and that at the beginning there was neither existence nor non-existence.

> Neither did non existence exist, nor did existence exist then;
>
> Neither did atmosphere exist, nor the skies beyond.
>
> what covered it? where? In whose protection?
>
> was there water, deep and impervious?

The ancient philosophy of Confucius was founded on the principles of humaneness and righteousness. Life is a continuous ordering of the polarities of yin and yang - disorder (negative) and order (positive). Together they form a mutual whole of the universe, which is created out of energy. The answer is to lead a life of the middle way. Here is an example of Confucian wisdom: 'Think of tomorrow, for the past can't be mended.'

The Old Testament has been profoundly influential upon all three Abrahamic faiths – Judaism, Christianity and Islam.

Here in Ecclesiastes 3 is an example of its timeless wisdom:

> There is a time for everything,
>
> And a season for every activity under heaven.
>
> A time to be born and a time to die,
>
> A time to plant and a time to uproot,
>
> A time to kill and a time to heal,
>
> A time to tear down and a time to build,
>
> A time to weep and a time to laugh,
>
> A time to mourn and a time to dance,
>
> A time to scatter stones and a time to gather them,
>
> A time to embrace and a time to refrain,
>
> A time to search and a time to give up,
>
> A time to keep and a time to throw away,
>
> A time to tear and a time to mend,
>
> A time to be silent and a time to speak,
>
> A time to love and a time to hate,
>
> A time for war and a time for peace.

In the thirteenth century the Christian theologian, Saint Thomas Aquinas wrote:

The intellectual soul is created on the boundary between time and

       Eternity. The way in which it acts to come into conjunction with

       Those higher things that are above time, participates in eternity…

       From this it follows that those who reach the ultimate bliss in the

       Divine vision cannot ever lose it.

We try to attain the Enlightenment of the Buddha:

       It is difficult to obtain the human state, difficult to live as a human,

       Difficult to accept Dharma, difficult to reach Enlightenment

There is an ancient Daoist verse:

       Before Heaven and Earth there existed something without differentiating

       Characteristics, complete in itself. Without either sound or form

       It is dependent on nothing and does not change. It is active everywhere and never fails.

       It acts as the mother of the universe. I do not know its

       Name. I call it Dao. The best I can do to name it is to call it Great.

       Humans follow the ways of Earth, Earth follows the ways of Heaven,

       Heaven follows the ways of Dao, Dao follows the ways of itself.

This is the opening sura of the Qur'an:

       In the name of God, the merciful Lord of mercy,

       Praise be to God, the Lord of all being,

       The merciful Lord of mercy,

       Sovereign of the Day of Judgment:

       You alone do we serve and to alone we come for help:

       Guide us in the straight path,

       The path of those on whom You have bestowed favour,

       Not of those against whom is the wrath,

       Nor of those who are straying in error.

And here is The Lord's Prayer:

       Our Father, which art in heaven

       Hallowed be thy Name.

       Thy Kingdom come.

Tea on the terrace

Thy will be done in earth,

As it is in heaven.

Give us this day our daily bread.

And forgive us our trespasses,

As we forgive them that trespass against us.

And lead us not into temptation,

But deliver us from evil.

For thine is the kingdom,

The power, and the glory,

For ever and ever.

Amen.

Even Heaven, supposed to be perfect, when visualized by humans is not immune to the conflict of physics. Revelation 12:7:

> And there was war in heaven. Michael and his angels fought against the dragon, and the dragon and his angels fought back. But he was not strong enough, and they lost their place in heaven. The great dragon was hurled down – that ancient serpent called the devil, or Satan, who leads the whole world astray. He was hurled to the earth, and his angels with him.

Francis has put his finger on it. As human beings feel physics happening inside themselves they invent stories (religions) to explain these feelings, to understand them – they are made 'romantic'.

Harari explains that *Homo sapiens* yearn for stories that we and our social group can believe in – as we bond together - for they give meaning to life. And the Christian myth is a powerful, emotionally moving story. But by a sleight of hand, Harari says, God, the cosmic mystery has transformed into God, the worldly lawgiver. This God is concerned with the minutiae of our daily lives and is woven into an elaborate Christian story which bonds 'believers', but excludes 'unbelievers' like Francis and me. These incredible stories emanate, I suggest, from the drama (the physical and emotional dynamics) within us and that is why sensible humanism (favoured by Harari and other thinkers like Steven Pinker and A C Grayling) does not, I fear, have the emotion and spirituality humans crave. We can see that religions arise from the powerful, conflicting feelings which humans feel internally, which mirror the two Laws of Thermodynamics. And this ongoing dynamic inside us is also, I suggest, evident in every ancient mythological tale and in every contemporary novel.

The universe within

'The only equivalent of the universe without is the universe within.' For 30 years Laurens van der Post explored his universe within, in the tiny middle room of our Lookout tower. He loved this little room because he could be alone with his imagination and write, and maybe also because, his mentor, Carl Jung, whose insight the universe within was, also wrote from a tower, on a lake near Zurich.

Van der Post absorbed the ideas of very many thinkers including this great psychiatrist and combined them, together with his own experience, in his inspirational writing. Here, van der Post is considering our human responsibility to the world and how through 'dreaming' (*zezing*) we can use our creativity to do something positive:

> It may be that there are other worlds with forms of being, with a greater awareness of this responsibility than we have, but this is what is on our doorstep and knocking so powerfully to be allowed in. For the moment this is our unique role. We have already got power enough to destroy the whole of human life; but have not yet got the moral obligation, the sense of good and bad, to match it and follow it as our instrument of metamorphosis. We have not yet accepted that every act of knowledge, every increase of knowledge, increases our responsibility towards creation. We have been induced into believing that we are completely helpless in the grip of powerful new forces and that we are caught up in a process that is meaningless, and just sweeping us along like a swine of a new Gadarene. But we have the power to be creative if we turn back to what I can only call 'the dreaming process' in ourselves, and we put our imaginations and our lives into this new area where the dream occurs; then we can 'do' and we can change life. (From A Walk with a White Bushman, 1986.)

In his life, van der Post was celebrated, knighted, mentor to both Prime Minister Margaret Thatcher and Prince Charles. But after his death a biographer found he was not as virtuous as he made out. (Who is?)

I answered 'maybe' to the third question in the Bishop's Christianity test: 'Is there an afterlife?' Where is Laurens van der Post now? In photos he is happy, smiling, playing tennis with Benjamin Britten. Where is BB now? Are they both in Hell? Card-carrying Christians (many of them hypocrites themselves we are now discovering) might say they hope so. I answered 'maybe' because maybe their ideas, the manifestation of their souls, live on in timelessness, in the collective unconscious, inspiring humankind in the 'tool chain of ideas' for eternity. Their bodies have returned, no doubt, to stardust.

This morning I am swimming; thinking of van der Post's 'dreaming process' and how through it we can change life. I am dreaming, or *zezing*. I prefer its positivity to mindfulness, for it uses First Law creative thinking, rather than passive Second Law body and mind maintenance. Concentrating on the present moment may be therapeutic for some, but on its own, for me, it's not enough, nor I respectfully conclude is praying to God (or the universe.)

Panoramic view from the top of the Lookout

But now the rhythm of my breaststroke dissolves all thoughts; I close my eyes and I am in Aristotelian Nowness.

Physics and metaphysics

Early each morning, in the magical space of the terrace overlooking the roaring sea with my squawking, over nosy friends for company, I write, in a stream of consciousness. This morning I am in the world of last night when I slept in the Lookout. Friends and I had sat having supper and chatting while we watched the beach and the sea and the sky change colour before us, like a psychedelic movie. When they left I couldn't bear to leave the drama, so, checking Francis was OK I put up a camp bed in there. Then I swam, as I sometimes do, late at night in the delicious blackness of the sea. I had been reading from Aristotle's *Metaphysics* during the day. In this book (which gives the philosophy of abstract, untestable concepts its name) this great thinker grappled with Plato's belief that the real nature of things is eternal and unchangeable, with his own naturalistic view (as Rovelli also says) that the world around us is constantly and perpetually changing. While I swam all of Aristotle's thoughts about being, knowing, identity, time and space were floating around inside me and a haiku began to form in my mind. When I got out of the sea I rushed, still wet, to write it down before it disappeared:

Time and timelessness
are where physics and metaphysics, become one.

Exactly seventeen syllables. I slept in the Lookout, with the doors open, underneath the stars, so I could feel close to the universe all night.

Now, this morning, I am again thinking about Aristotle. When he was not thinking about Now, he realized that each person needs to lead a flourishing life. Surprisingly or unsurprisingly, so often our idiosyncratic personal life-skills and experiences seem to converge, to help us, as I have found. Who would have thought *Protestantism and the spirit of Capitalism*, part of my 'dull' sociology degree, would now be so fascinating to me and relevant; or that my barrister skills would be so needed to argue my case (that the thermodynamic laws of the universe govern us every moment as time and timelessness, and we experience them as the pressure of everyday life and as a feeling of transcendence) or that my Bunny Girl waitressing skills learnt at London's Playboy Club would be so useful for pouring drinks at the opening of *Einstein and Picasso: Revolutionaries in Time and Space* last Saturday?

Ideas for eternity

A friend has analysed me. Immersing myself in the sea is, he believes, a metaphor for immersing myself in my

View towards the North Lookout

subconscious. I think he is right. And the chance and indifference of its personality is the chance and indifference of C S Lewis's godless world, into which I venture each day. While swimming this morning the sea became too pesky, so I could not *zez*, because I need not to worry about drowning when I turn off my conscious mind. So I scrambled out pronto, and as I showered my thoughts moved back to Aristotle. His thoughts about our livelihood being our unique purpose were particularly insightful because then no one had any concept of creativity or evolution. Now we appreciate how indebted we are to human creativity. For example, as I dressed, a choice – which skirt, which trousers? Trousers – straight out of Tommy Hilfiger's soul. 'Creativity is dragging from your soul an idea,' said this entrepreneur of clothing.

I leaf through Francis's newspaper while he drinks his coffee. Yet more examples of how human beings change life for the better through their creativity. How to enable a paralysed man to regain use of his limbs (a scientific, creative solution, not a miracle) and another, how to get every last bit out of the ketchup bottle (a serious problem, not only to each of us personally but also to mankind, for it causes wastage on a global scale). Someone has just invented a slippery inside to the bottle.

Now with my staple cup of camomile in hand, I walk around the house doing jobs. Creativity is what makes us human - I remember Bronowski, as I take the washing from the dryer and upstairs for ironing. Why, I wonder? Interestingly, creativity is the only function of the brain whose unpredictability is integral to its success. Thus this most precious bit of our brain is not replaceable by artificial intelligence, which relies on pre-programming with predictive algorithms. I am looking in the fridge thinking about what (not much) we have for lunch. Maybe it is precisely because we experience time (memory, now, anticipation) that we *Homo sapiens* can be so supremely creative?   We each have creative energy inside us, waiting to be activated, and the challenge for each of us is to transform it into something very personal and valuable to add to creation. Over the nearly ten years I have been here I have studied the lives of creatively successful, ie fulfilled people, and interestingly, have found that invariably, they have certain conditions in their lives, which enable their creativity to blossom. These necessary conditions, fascinatingly, form an algorithm, which I call creative intelligence or CQ.

Now, after our somewhat meagre lunch, I am chopping peppers for Picasso's favourite omelette while I listen to the radio, hearing a woman talk about the anger she feels; she knows, she says, she has no control over her life. 'Life's all about feeling in control over our lives, which we gain through discovering our unique creativity,' I say (politely, of course) to the radio.

Realizing infinity

Today is the hottest ever recorded in England. It's been like this for a couple of weeks. As I tried to sleep in this heat last night, I was thinking of the eggs to be scrambled, and how I will, inadvertently, be adding to the universe's entropy because scrambling disorders the eggs' molecules irreversibly. More seriously, is entropy winning over creativity, no matter how virtuous or creative we are?

I won't think about that now. The sea is like a Mediterranean lake, without a ripple, and as I swim I am asking why it is we need artistic creativity. I understand creativity for practical, economic ends, of course, for creativity is the ultimate source of all economic value and innovation. But why do artists spend all week in our little tower for no obvious benefit? The philosopher-theologian Paul Tillich concluded it is to communicate a shared sense of humanity (so we trade peacefully together, I would add). Creative ideas combine to form the collective conscious, which we call culture, and through culture, society can hold many more ideas in its collective mind than any one person can. Culture forms the moral and social rules physics needs societies to live by. 'A nation's culture resides in the hearts and souls of its people', Gandhi said. The British artist Mat Collishaw puts it another way: 'I hope nothing comes after art. Without art we become inhuman; we could become very dangerous animals without literature and pictures and music and all those things which share tenderness and anger and the complex experience of being human.'

I do make Einstein's scrambled eggs and serve them together with Picasso's omelette niçoise for our closing party. It's full of artists having fun. Artists are particularly practised at being 'in the zone' or 'in the flow.' But it's not only artists and other creatives who experience this sensation – when time seems to stand still. As we focus doing whatever we enjoy most, we create thoughts and ideas - which are complex matter. Matter makes time slow down and this I suggest, is how we creative animals help the universe hold back time, even if only marginally. We are a tiny pinpoint of order within the increasingly disordered universe as entropy slows down inside us and we feel this physics within as time slowing down. It is profoundly pleasurable and addictive. Whoever we are, when we are in the midst of being our true, creative self, however we express it, we feel this timelessness, *kairos*.

We may also experience this sense of timelessness through intense religious devotion, *ekstasis*, or spiritual awe or through meditation. This state of altered consciousness, called transcendence by some, was for T S Eliot, the way for people to search for God. Our conscious existence, as Eliot expressed through his epic poem, *The Four Quartets*, is the point of intersection between time and timelessness.

> A people without history
> Is not redeemed from time, for history is a pattern
> Of timeless moments

I urge us to strive to experience timelessness through discovering our unique creativity. For then we are in control of our own fascinating and meaningful life story, rather than passively accepting the incredible, often unhelpful, ones of others. We can embark on our personal spiritual journey to eternity through our creativity. But we have to bear in mind that salvation is not 'certain', as religions promise; for the creative option in life can be tortuous and has no guarantee of success.

Yet we *Homo sapiens* are programmed to subject ourselves to the elation and despair which is part and parcel of our creative urge. And for most of the artists who come to Aldeburgh this is a spiritual journey towards… what? Salvation? Heaven? Eternity? Maggi Hambling, like Benjamin Britten before her, draws her emotions from the roaring Aldeburgh sea: 'Art is talking to God,' she says. 'Painting and religious experience are the same thing,' said the modern British artist, Ben Nicholson: 'What we are all searching for is the understanding and realisation of infinity.' Creativity is also the path to spirituality for the artist Sean Scully: 'Religion has to a very large degree in our society been replaced by art. I am looking for a new kind of religious feeling without the tragedy of dogma and all the grief it's caused.' The Turner prize-winner, self-styled 'transvestite potter' Grayson Perry puts it his way: 'Art is spirituality in drag.'

For when we have art which is purposefully unspiritual, as Terry Eagleton describes Postmodernism, it can be blamed, he says, for opening up a spiritual void which political or religious fundamentalism can invade: 'Postmodernism with its notorious absence of effect is post-numinous,' he writes, in *Culture and the Death of God*.

That evening, Francis and I are having supper watching the news, and tears fall down my cheeks. How wonderful is the human race that we link together across our selfish thermodynamic clusters, and combine our creativity to save 12 Thai boys trapped in an underground cave. The next news item is about humans killing other humans, as usual. We need art, as Mat Collishaw says.

Becoming

Next morning swimming is divinely refreshing, although the littoral, usually nearly people- less, has turned into Brighton beach. The artist duo Miche Fabre Lewin and Flora Gathorne-Hardy have a residency in our tower this week. They have set up a beautifully thought-out project in the Lookout called *Life of Water*, which demonstrates how art can be a powerful way of communicating important messages, in their case that water is a most precious commodity, with its own life which we must treasure.

Before we open I sit on the terrace in the morning cool, with my loyal feathery friends for company. From Nowness to Becoming. Becoming, I read, was the favourite word of an Englishman, Alfred North Whitehead, living in America at the same time that T S Eliot, the American, was living in England.

> The conclusion is that in every act of becoming there is the becoming of something with temporal extension; but the act itself is not extensive, in the sense that it is divisible into earlier and later acts of becoming which correspond to the extensive divisibility of what has become.

Both Whitehead and Eliot thought deeply about time and timelessness, and also about God. For T S Eliot, whose poetry laments the nihilism of the First World War, and the poignancy of time, God was the sense of order he needed outside his suffering self. (Eliot suffered great personal sadness from his unhappy marriage, and from sexual difficulties.) He loved the tradition and ritual and emotion of Anglo Catholicism. But Eliot's was not an impotent belief in an all-powerful Creator but as a way we can all participate in life. For Whitehead, God is found in possibility, which is expressed through human creativity and individual freedom. Whitehead and Eliot knew each other but did not always concur, for – because of his unhappiness – Eliot needed the support of a personalized religion. Whitehead's God was more abstract.

For Whitehead, as he set out to demonstrate, life consists of interconnecting creative processes in every atom in our bodies (similar to Rovelli's description) and this, for Whitehead, is our experience of God inside us. Aged 63, this very English mathematician was invited to Harvard as Professor of Philosophy. He used his position there to explore the microbiology of our cells and in particular their quantum vacuum where minute quanta exist in timelessness, of zero heat. From there these tiny quanta pop in and out of existence unpredictably, and some have the possibility of being created in the positive process which leads on to evolution through the First Law of Thermodynamics, the transformation of energy. For Whitehead, that place of timelessness inside the quantum vacuum, which offers the possibility of creation, is where we find God. Just as we experience the physics of time, so we experience the physics of creation, God, happening inside our atoms.

In search of lost time

Behind a chair in Francis' room I find a complete set of Proust. Like so many of his generation (he is 14 years older than me) Francis read the entirety of *In Search of Lost Time* and he dedicated months to this Proustian task:

> When a distant past nothing subsists, after people are dead, after the destruction of things alone, more fragile but more enduring, more unsubstantial, more persistent, more faithful, the smell and flavour are still long, like souls, remembering, waiting, hoping, the ruin of everything else, and bear unfaltering, in their impalpable droplet, the immense edifice of memory.
> From: *In Search of Lost Time (Swann's Way)*

Proust's close relation by marriage, the French philosopher Henri Bergson, was engaged in intense intellectual discussions about time with Alfred North Whitehead as well as with Proust, T S Eliot, Bertrand Russell and other eminent philosophers of the day, some of whom criticised him for considering intuition as important as science. But intuition, maybe they forgot, was vital to the key discoveries of both Einstein and Darwin, which were not scientifically proved until later.

Staircase descending a Nude by mmmmm, projected onto the Lookout

A tiny art temple

Today is steaming hot again, and I am again on the terrace. I look down to the Lookout which is looking very pretty thanks to Miche and Flora. They have brought in cushions, and bowls of cucumbers and fruits from Flora's kitchen garden; and covered the old plinths with checked tablecloths on which they have placed jugs and glasses of water samples (sewage, used bath, sea, river, rain, tap) positioned as art.

There is a refreshing breeze up here and so I linger and look through a well-loved book that Flora reminded me of. Jim Ede wrote about setting up Kettle's Yard, his house of art in Cambridge. He was an inspiration to me, and our house here and the Lookout is the result. Ede supported artists some of whom went on to great acclaim. It moves me to remember the artists who have come here over our eight years (well over a hundred of them it must be) from established Royal Academicians like Nigel Hall, Eileen Cooper, Alison Wilding, Anne Desmet, Chris Orr, Stephen Farthing and Anthony Green to the young and emerging. Some of them are already achieving great success. For example, Clara Drummond credits her residency at the Lookout with the development of her drawing style so that she went on to win the BP Portrait Prize in 2016.

One of our first visitors to the Lookout was Richard Demarco. He, like Sir Peter Blake, was amongst the first to encourage Francis and me to take on this adventure. Peter had known this little tower from years ago when he came to Aldeburgh and made a collage inscribed in his handwriting 'A five minute walk along the beach on a bitterly cold winter morning,' and he kindly made a print of it as a fundraiser for us. Richard climbed to the top of the Lookout and, on seeing the view from shore to horizon, roared in his broad Scottish accent: 'New beginnings are in the offing!' quoting Joseph Beuys. After the second world war Richard realised that art was a way of healing wounds and brought Beuys, young and iconoclastic, from Germany to Scotland. Beuys broadened the definition of art: 'Life is art,' he said, 'every living being is an artist - an artist in the sense that he can develop his own capacity. Each person is a unique participant in one social sculpture.'

This insight has been our founding principle.

Poets come here - Annie Freud, Blake Morrison, George Szirtes... 31 of them have written poetry in the tower. Ian McMillan calls the beach and the Lookout 'a kind of poetic paradise.... The moment of climbing the rickety ladder to gaze from the window at the sea is comparable to the moment when a poem begins to resolve itself in your head: there is a flash or clarity, followed by a clamber down to where the real work begins.'

John Cage's riotous Musicircus was happening all around us one Aldeburgh Festival, and we contributed to it by playing Erik Satie's *Vexations* 840 times. So, non-stop, over 18 hours our rota of pianists played Francis's grand piano in the first-floor drawing room, with the balcony doors wide open so all on the sea-front could hear. We boiled 840 eggs for exactly 4 minutes 33 seconds (each with a face painted on it by the artist Liza Adamczewski) and Ian wrote a poem about it:

The John Cage Egg by Ian McMillan

Now bring to the boil; listen, listen hard
As the bubbles burst suddenly, steam rises

Making silent shapes in the receptive air,
And the egg itself knocks rhythm, rhythms

Against the unthinking pan. The egg hardens
Into the kind of silence you can eat,

The kind of silence you can bring soldiers to,
The kind of silence you can put in, yes, an egg cup

And tap with a spoon. Resonant silence,
The best kind. Turn the egg-timer, slowly:

Boil the egg for exactly 4 minutes, 33 seconds;
No less, no more. Exact, exacting silence.

We have had fun here, and still do, but 'The John Cage Egg' was earlier in time, some six months before Francis's accident, and he was one of the rota of *Vexations* pianists. The cultural supremo Humphrey Burton was another. He and the beautiful actress Diana Quick have been wonderfully supportive of our creative extravaganzas, and they are patrons of our Arts Club Aldeburgh Beach which is, we like to think, a combination of the Chelsea Arts Club and Gertrude Stein's art salon.

A new Arts Club member is Jenny Hall, who, like her late father Sir Peter Hall, finds Shakespeare timelessly fascinating. She chose this sonnet about time, for us.

Like as the waves make towards the pebbl'd shore,
So do minutes hasten to their end;
Each changing place with that which goes before,
In sequent toil all forwards do contend.

Einstein said that art is the profoundest thought expressed in the simplest way, and I hope and think our artists achieve this. Each, like Margaret Koval, turns the Lookout into their creative home for a week and makes wonderful, always surprising, works of art. And many of these works hang in our home, this house, the

Blake Morrison launching his book of poetry. Our next door neighbours Janice Turner and Ben Preston with their John Cage eggs.
and furnished with his crucifixions and kitsch knick-knacks. 40 Bedlington terriers also attended the launch on that freezing March da
Macdonald install *Murmuration* as part of Poetry in Aldeburgh, 2016. Annie Freud and 30 other poets at the launch of the Lookout: P
seconds precisely, and with faces drawn on each by the artist Liza Adamczewski. Ian McMillan wrote the John Cage egg.

Laste launches her monograph on Craigie Aitchison. For a monthe the Lookout was recreated as Craigie's sitting room - painted pink, then we all (including the dogs) ate fish and chips inside the Lookout. Tom Hiddleston with his John Cage egg. Sarah Wood and Helen from Aldeburgh Beach again in 2016. Michael Horovitz and Vanessa Vie in mid performance. 840 eggs each boiled for 4 mins and 33

Arthouse, which, some say, is like a living, breathing Kettle's Yard by the sea. And the Lookout is, as Miche and Flora say, a tiny art temple.

The creative journey to eternity

The opening of *Life of Water* was a great success yesterday.

But this morning, Sunday, it is freezing and blowing a gale. Despite our awkward bed arrangement, we cuddle while we listen to our favourite Sunday morning programmes – spirituality through dancing; making a living, living with pigs; the usual clergy paedophilia – and *Sunday Worship* is about St Francis of Assisi.

We and all animals and insects are linked in God's creation, and are interdependent. That is Francis of Assisi's message. I agree (but might substitute the word universe for god).

> All creatures of our God and king
> Lift up your voices and with us sing
> Alleluia, alleluia
> Thou burning with golden beam
> Thou silver moon with softer gleam
> Alleluia, alleluia, alleluia, alleluia, alleluia.

We are singing, quietly. I kiss Francis's hair and, like Proust, I remember…

It's next day, Monday, the Aldeburgh Carnival. The sun has come out and every one is in a good mood. Francis and I are alone together as I push him along Crag Path, with jollity happening all around us. I sit down on a bench enjoying the warmth on my face, and then look into Francis's face, still craggily handsome (although I haven't trimmed his eyebrows.) It has been over eight years since we set ourselves quests. For Francis it was to explore and respond to life by discovering for himself his 'emotional explanation of the universe', just as E M Forster challenged himself, in conversation with Benjamin Britten, here on Aldeburgh beach some 70 years ago. For me it was that and, very specifically, to understand that fascinating enigma, human creativity. Change has happened since then, and time and timelessness have intervened.

Interestingly, it was through using creative thinking that I found, what I believe to be, significant breakthroughs in our understanding of the phenomenon of creativity itself. Zezing as I swam in the sea each morning, I could combine contrasting ideas from philosophy, physics, and theology, which are normally kept separate, and come up with brand new propositions about what it is to be human.

Francis and me in the Arthouse the year before his accident. Behind us are works by Bill Jackson and Chris Orr RA

I want so much to talk through these new thoughts about life with the old Francis, for he would surely have challenged me with perceptive thoughts of his own. But as it is, as we sit together in our own world, on the sea front that Carnival afternoon, I test them out on the new, more easy-going Francis.

'Its almost,' I began, somewhat shyly, 'it's as if… through our evolved highly sophisticated consciousness, we humans are given the privilege of co-creating with the universe.' I took a deep breath: 'Because, I suggest, it's our uniquely human awareness of time which is key to our creativity, which is so incredibly efficient because it collaborates, through the collective subconscious, with all of creation.' He looked towards me, so I ventured on. 'Our personal creativity is fuelled, as is all of creation, by the universe's drive to order energy into matter - this Carnival, for instance, which is a fabulous and fun manifestation of human creative energy.' We were looking at the children laughing as they rode up and down on fairground horses, and then further into the distance at the beauty of the whiteness and roundness of Sizewell Nuclear Power station. 'And, you know what, Francis? I've just realised something. Einstein's equation $E = Mc^2$ states this precisely. It describes the interchangeability of energy and matter.' Francis was looking at me again now. 'The transformation of energy into matter, this ordering of energy, conserves it and so slows down the growth of disordered energy, which we experience as time, and which will, in time, bring the end of time, and death to the universe and everything in it.'

I looked into the depths of those greeny, brown eyes, which for me contain within them the entirety of the mystery of the universe. 'The universe needs us.' I said. 'And in response, we feel a special, romantic - that was your word, Francis - relationship with it. And this religious feeling encourages us to co-create most efficiently, or "perfectly" as that vicar on the radio urged me.' I searched his face for clues, whether he was understanding or agreeing or disagreeing. 'And as we struggle every day with those two onerous and conflicting laws of physics inside us, we feel loved because we are needed by the universe.'

'Some people,' Francis was speaking so quietly I could barely hear, 'might call this God's love?'

I drew his blanket over him a little, as there was a chilly sea breeze even on this August afternoon. 'Well, I think so,' I said, and kissed his smooth cheek.

'And the universe…' I had nearly finished, 'encourages our intense creative efforts with transcendent timeless moments and we are rewarded with a sense of fulfilment and meaning to life. And this keeps us carrying on, just as you did, Francis, helping the universe in its monumental task of holding back the end of time.'

Then, as time moves through the afternoon and we sit huddled a little closer, the merriment of the Carnival escalating around us, I ask Francis about his quest: Has he found his emotional explanation of the universe? 'It is to contribute to life,' he said. 'You have, and still are,' I reassured him. 'And to enjoy it,' he continued, unexpectedly. Taken aback, I asked him something I have never dared to broach since the day the accident devastated his mind and body. 'Are you still enjoying life, Francis?'

I read his lips. 'I am,' he said, softly.

An emotional explanation of the universe

For some, perhaps influenced by Plato, God is timelessness above the universe, with us, his creation, inside the rule of time. And some find God at the microscopic quantum level, as Whitehead described, at the timeless birth of creation. Some physicists propose that the universe may itself have emerged out of one large quantum vacuum. Quantum theory is described sometimes as 'cloudy and fitful' which is not unlike 'the cloud of unknowing', an anonymous medieval monk's description of God. God for Einstein was the wonder of this cosmic mystery. He, like Steve and so many other scientists, was constantly struck with awe at the beauty of the universe we live in. It had a beginning, Stephen Hawking tells us, and thus before the big bang, time did not exist. Over 3,000 years ago ancient Vedic religions intuited this same scientific conclusion – at the beginning was the void, God, timelessness.

Maybe the secret of the mystery of the universe lies deep within us, as eternal elements of its infinity, as co-creators; and as artists, as we all are with our new, broad, Beuysian definition. The job of the artist, said the twentieth-century painter Francis Bacon, 'is always to deepen the mystery'.

Oh, and Morgan (if, Mr Forster, I may call you by your fore name) if I should come across your soul on Aldeburgh beach one misty morning, I have my emotional explanation of the universe to offer you:

> **The wondrous ability of human beings to co-create with the universe by transforming our unique creative energy into something to benefit humanity, and thereby contribute to the eternity of the universe.**

Credits

Front end paper - Regine Bartsch detail of *Time Again (Aldeburgh Beach),* mixed media on canvas
Back end paper - Lee Maeltzer: close up of moss growing on a window ledge, inside the Lookout

Photography credits

Kitchen - James Balston
The terrace - James Balston
My study - James Balston
Tea on the terrace - James Balston
View towards North Lookout - James Balston
Panorama from the top of the Lookout - Nick Sinclair
The lady in the tower - Bill Jackson
Lookout at night - Bambina Carnwath
Photograph of Caroline Wiseman (back cover) and various other photographs - Amanda Houchen
Various photographs - Janieve Crompton

First published February 2020 by Lookout Editions, Alive in the Universe
31 Crag Path, Aldeburgh, Suffolk, IP15 5BS. UK
caroline@aliveintheuniverse.com
www.aliveintheuniverse.com

ISBN 978 0 9962625 01 3

A CIP record for this book is available from the British Library.

Design and typesetting by Karen Delaney

Printed and bound by Healeys Printers, Ipswich